Creative papier maché

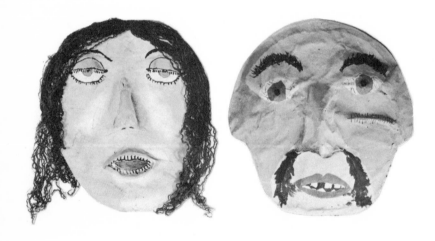

Creative
papier maché

Betty Lorrimar

WATSON-GUPTILL PUBLICATIONS / NEW YORK

Acknowledgements

I would like to thank Margaret Hickson for all her help, advice and encouragement. I also wish to acknowledge the inspiration provided by the students of Maidenhead High School, who produced such stimulating and creative work.

I am also grateful for help received from the following:

Mr and Mrs S. Cheyney; The Victoria and Albert Museum, London, for permission to reproduce furniture in their collection — figs 8, 20, 83, 96–7, 99, 101; The Commonwealth Institute for fig. 100; The Pitt Rivers Museum, Oxford for figs 61–2; The Museum of Childhood, Edinburgh, for figs 1, 31–2, 53–55, 80, 98; The Atelier Keiser, Frankfurt/Main for figs 4–7; The Hanover Gallery, London, for figs 56, 102. Also S. Vea Advertising Agency, Stockholm, for fig. 50 — Creative Director, Bjorn Petersson; Art Director, Bengt Good; Photograph, Goran Bjorling.

Manufactured in U.S.A.

ISBN 0-8230-1096-1

Library of Congress Catalog Card Number: 74-114196

First Printing, 1971

Contents

Introduction   7
List of materials   9
   Essential   9
   Useful items   9
   Finishing materials   11
Painting papier maché   12
Decoration by découpage   13
Other methods of decorating   18
Moulded objects   20
   How to begin   21
   Decorating   23
Making maracas   26
Making trays   28
Bottle figures   30
   Decoration   35
Toys   36
Small figures and animals   38
   Free, loose paper modelling   45
Large figures   46
How to make paper pulp   52
Sculpture   55
Masks   60
Puppets   64
Scenery and stage properties   67
Decorative flowers   71
Jewellery   73
   Ways of making beads   74
   Bracelets and earrings   74
   Pendants, brooches and rings   75
Dolls   76
Boxes   78
Hats and hat stands   80
   The hat stand   83
Umbrella stands, wastepaper baskets   84
Lampshades   86
Furniture   87
Origin and uses of papier maché   92
List of suppliers   102
For further reading   103
Index   104

Fig. 1   Indian wind tiger (nodding head), *c.* 1930. Museum of Childhood, Edinburgh

Introduction

Man has always needed three-dimensional expression, and papier maché is one of the cheapest and most easily-obtained materials that he can use. It is based on the principle that paper mixed with paste becomes hard when it is dry. Papier maché takes various forms — it can be a modelling pulp; a thin shell placed over a mould; or it can be pasted, crumpled and freely shaped. It is a craft that can be enjoyed by all age groups — working as individuals, or combining on large-scale projects. Imagination is stimulated and fully used. There is excitement in deciding what to create, then planning the best way to do it. This is a useful exercise in itself, great freedom is possible in the preliminary modelling or moulding, careful craftsmanship must follow — joins, creases and other weak points need tidying up. Lastly there is the decoration to be embarked upon. The surface can be covered by a great variety of materials, or decorated with paint. Many decisions must be taken. Everyone becomes really engrossed, and all stages of mental ability can be satisfied. Messy people can have a delightful time being untidy, but happy in the knowledge that papier maché is one of the easiest materials to clear up. Neat workers can be satisfied too, as there is really no need to make a mess!

The substance is very pliable, and delicate and bold results are both possible. In school, work can be for sheer creative pleasure or it can be used as a link with several subjects. Geography and history are obvious choices, with rich scenes to be modelled. Papier-maché puppets can be used in English lessons, either to act out plays written by the children, or to see how well they can interpret a literary character when making a model. Masks for use in drama and modern-dance lessons can also be made quite easily. It is of course possible to achieve some grotesque results, but even these may have their charm. In any case, the stimulation of creating something is always a worthwhile exercise. The majority of paintings produced in an art class are usually only fit for the rubbish bin, but they have not been a waste of time. The children will have been lost in a world of their own while mixing colours and brushing them onto paper to create some wonderful scene or pattern. So it is with papier maché. It is one of the most adaptable materials to use, and can help to develop an appreciation of form and encourage ideas, as well as provide a really enjoyable form of craftwork which does not need expensive equipment or materials.

List of materials

Essential

Paper Newspapers are pliable, easy to obtain and make excellent pulp. Other papers can be used – paper towels, lining paper, crepe paper. Paper tissues etc. are useful when small, fine work is wanted. Magazines are not usually suitable, as they are often hard and brittle – particularly the more expensive kind.

Paste Cellulose paste is recommended, as it keeps well, but other types may be used. Decorators' paste, starch, cold-water paste supplied in powder form, and flour paste all work well. To make flour paste, mix a tablespoonful of flour with cold water to make a smooth cream. Pour on boiling water, stirring as you do so. The mixture will change its texture and appear transparent. Allow to cool. A few drops of oil of cloves will preserve the paste, but this need not be added if the paste is to be used within two or three days. Make starch as for laundry, but rather thickly.

Container A bucket will hold a large quantity of paste. A pudding bowl, mixing bowl or jug may be used. The main point to consider is that it must have a wide top, so that paper can be dipped in easily.

Useful items

Paints These may be any type – watercolours, oils or acrylics, enamels, emulsions, in fact the entire range available for art work.

Fig. 2 *Teenager* by Anne White and Anne Wilks, aged 14. This model is life-size and made entirely of paper. The base is made from large, tightly-rolled newspaper tubes. These were covered with several layers of paper strips. The clothing is made from sheets of newsprint dipped in paste and then modelled to the figure. The guitar is of cardboard. The spectacles are pink cellophane with cardboard surround. Poster colours were used to paint this 'pop' character

Brushes Again these can be of any kind.

Scissors For cutting patterns, découpage, and making clothing for models, *not* for cutting paper to make mash.

Cottons, needles, pins and other needlework accessories.

Strong glue White synthetic glue is best, sold in liquid form, Copydex, Evostik are good (in U.S., use Sobo).

Cardboard Plain or corrugated will do. Old grocery cartons are useful.

Box of scrap materials This should include as large a variety of things as possible – string, wool (yarn), feathers, raffia, tinfoil, beads, buttons, all types of fabric. This is one of the sources of inspiration when decorating models.

Gummed tape Any type will do, although the self-adhesive kind is quicker and easier to use.

Wire Chicken wire and other wires of different thicknesses are very useful for armatures, especially when making large objects.

Plasticine or clay These can be used for basic modelling when making masks or puppets.

Gesso This is a mixture of whiting or Plaster of Paris and glue. It produces a plastic material which gives a good surface for painting on, or it may be left as a rather pleasing white finish. It can be sandpapered smooth and finally rubbed by hand to give a smooth, slightly shiny effect. Gesso can be bought ready to use, but may be made as follows: mix equal quantities of whiting and water. Do not stir, as this causes bubbles. Leave to stand for a few minutes. Pour off any excess water. Add a half quantity of glue – any liquid type may be used, but white synthetic glue is best. Add a few drops of linseed oil. The mixture may now be gently stirred. It should be like thick cream; if it is too thin, add more whiting; if too thick, more water. It is now ready for applying to the papier maché.

Finishing materials

Varnish is a good waterproof protective finish. It may be bought shiny or matt, but make sure that it is transparent. Several layers may be used to give a durable surface. Wax polish, transparent floor polish or car polish can be rubbed over the models. This is not as lasting as varnish, but gives a soft pleasing shine to objects.

Laquer is most often used in papier-maché work. It is quick drying and gives a hard finish. It may be bought to give a matt or glossy finish.

Fig. 3   Some useful items for the papier-maché artist. Only three things are really needed – paste, paper and colour – but other equipment, as seen here, can be useful. String, gummed tape, Plasticine, white glue, wire and varnish are among the objects

Painting papier maché

Most types of paint can be used to cover the material, but certain precautions should be taken. A coat of white emulsion paint brushed over the papier maché makes an excellent base. The white helps the other colours to appear fresh and glowing. This preliminary coat also seals the surface, and if you make a mistake when decorating with water-based colours, you can wash off easily without damaging the papier maché.

If oil paint is to be used, the surface must be sealed or the paint will dry unevenly and more coats will be required. Emulsion can be used for this, but other sealers are glue size, whiting or a prepared gesso. The preliminary emulsion is not absolutely essential when using poster colours, but has the advantages already mentioned. Do not use this type of colour too thickly, or it will crack.

Probably the best medium to use is acrylic paint, as this can be painted either thickly or thinly over most surfaces.

When the objects or models have been painted, they can be protected from dampness or marking by putting a coat of clear varnish or transparent matt varnish over them. Polishing with beeswax polish is also successful. Make sure the model is completely dry before polishing, and apply the beeswax slowly and carefully if you are covering watercolour paint, as some colours are inclined to smear. Lacquer is widely used as a finish too. Enamel paints give a good waterproof surface and do not require varnishing. Several thin layers are better than one or two thick ones. Gold paint and coloured lacquers are also effective. These are all unsuitable for small children to use, as brushes, hands and clothing are difficult to clean!

If you wish to avoid painting models, the final layer of paper can be put on in a decorative way. Tissue paper is produced in beautiful colours and is most attractive when different tones overlap in freely-shaped torn pieces. Sugar paper (cheap drawing paper) may also be used for the last layer, and it too can be obtained in a number of colours. Varnish or lacquer may be applied when dry to give waterproofing and protection to the surface.

Decoration by découpage

This term comes from the French language, and the dictionary defines it as the art of cutting. It is a skilled art, one must choose what to cut and plan the composition of the design. It is a fascinating method, and difficult to stop once one gets started! Decoration was skillfully done in this way during the eighteenth century in Europe. In some examples it is so well disguised that it has been mistaken for painting. Papier-maché furniture was frequently decorated by découpage. Cut-out flowers were covered by many layers of transparent lacquer, so that they appeared to be painted. In découpage the design is assembled completely from cut-outs. They can be large and bold, or fragile and lace-like. Sometimes very fine, detailed pictures are cut with a sharp knife rather than with scissors.

Another variation in cut-work decoration is called montage. In this découpage may be used as a background, or to enhance the montage additions. These are actual objects, and may be postage stamps, pressed flowers, cards and similar things. Trompe d'oeil is another form of découpage. This is also a French term, and means fooling the eye. This method can be amusing in a light hearted or a grim way. Realistic cut-outs of objects may be stuck onto furniture and appear to be falling out of drawers. Other pictures may show objects on a shelf — a skull, beads hanging from a nail etc. There are many examples of découpage decoration to be seen in old houses, antique shops and museums. Some countries specialized in the use of botanical objects combined with birds, insects and ribbons. These are usually exquisitely coloured. Swedish découpage is almost in monochrome but is very beautiful. Portuguese examples are different. They are gay and bright, using tinsel and brilliantly-coloured papers.

Today there is a wide choice of materials — for instance seed catalogues and magazines are easily obtained. Designs are usually bolder than those of the past, and very colourful. For those who are nervous at the thought of painting their papier-maché objects, découpage is the answer.

Fig. 4

Figs 4–7
Four examples of papier maché decorated by découpage which were used to advertize a furniture store in Geneva. This lively and arresting design, by the Studio Keiser, Frankfurt, shows the trend towards obtaining a three-dimensional effect in modern publicity. Of interest too is the way the pictures explain very simply the stages in creating a paper head as well as suggesting how to build up a home

Fig. 5

Fig. 6

Fig. 7

Other methods of decorating

Dolls and models are often decorated with materials and other sorts of collage. It is important to select carefully; if patterned cloth is to be used, see that it is correct in scale for the model. Also colours and textures should be chosen to blend well together. It is possible to make one's own exciting materials. One way is to produce batik patterns, either on paper or on cloth. Batik uses the principle of the resistance of wax to water. All you need do is to paint a design with liquid wax polish or draw with wax crayons. Melted beeswax or candles can be used, but this is a dangerous method for young children, as wax becomes very hot and easily flares up if spilt on the heater.

If working on paper, watercolour is now brushed over the entire surface. It will remain only on the unwaxed parts. The pattern may be left in one colour or have further colours applied. These are put on after more wax has been painted. If material is being treated, dyes are used instead of paint. The cold-water types are best, though others may be used if allowed to cool before brushing on the dye or dipping the fabric into the dye container. When the decoration has been completed in wax and colour, the paper or cloth will be very stiff, because of the wax. To remove this, newspaper is placed both below and above the design and a warm iron is run over. The wax will be seen to come onto the paper. Fresh pieces of newsprint should be put over and under and the iron used again. This process is repeated until all the wax is removed. Making patterned cloth or paper to use on models is fun to do, and gives them an even more individual character.

The batik method can also be applied directly to papier maché, to produce pleasing results. After a model has been finished and coated with white emulsion or poster colour, wax can be painted on. Any form of watercolour may then be brushed over and the wax will form a resist. A wax polish can be used as a protective finish. This type of decoration is suitable for hats, lampshades, models and moulded objects. A related way of creating a pattern on either cloth or paper is by tie dying, or folding and dying.

When using paper, the sheets are folded into pleats, diagonals or other folds. Parts of the paper are then dipped into watercolours or inks. The colour will spread a little but, if care is taken, it will not go over the whole thing. When unfolded, an interesting design will be seen. Absorbent papers are best for this method — newsprint, paper towels, or tissues. Cloth is tied into folds as tightly as possible and dipped into dye. It should be removed quickly and rinsed immediately. When untied fascinating patterns are discovered. The resist in this method is not wax but tight tying and folding.

Other ways of decorating papier maché are constantly evolving, as it is a living craft. In the past, mother-of-pearl was used extensively as an inlay. The chair illustrated here (fig. 8) is a fine example. It gives a rich, beautiful effect on the black background and is combined with floral motifs. Coloured strings can be applied all over the surface of models, to give a pleasing colour and texture.

The tones of newspaper pictures may also be used to great effect. The scenic flats shown in fig. 71 are examples of this.

Fig. 8 Chair of papier maché, mid-nineteenth century. Victoria and Albert Museum, London

Moulded objects

Obviously it is wise to begin with the simplest form of papier-maché modelling. Using a mould is an easy method. Plates are good objects to use, and trays, tin lids and pudding bowls are all suitable. Plastic bowls are also excellent because when the papier maché is dry it is easy to remove it from the flexible base. Always remember that the mould should be a larger shape at the top than the bottom, so that you can remove the article easily. Check that there are no undercuts to prevent you removing the papier maché.

Fig. 9 *Bowl* by Elizabeth Temple-Murray, aged 11. This was modelled over a plastic washing-up bowl. About eight layers of pasted paper were put over. The pattern is bold and free, painted in pink and purple poster colour. It is a strong bowl which could be used to hold fruit, or merely to be decorative

How to begin

The inside or outer surface of the mould can be used. Grease — vaseline or something similar — may be applied first, so that separation is easy at the later stage, but a layer of wet paper put on first works just as well. Scissors must not be used, the paper must always be torn. You will find it easier to tear straight pieces when going in the direction of the grain of the paper, as with fabrics. Do not use the cut edges of the newspaper, tear them off before you begin.

Strips of newspaper are put on in even layers. To facilitate counting the layers, and to help to obtain a uniform thickness, tissue paper can alternate with newsprint. Another way of checking is to change the direction of the type for the different layers. If you wish the article to be really strong, butter muslin (or cheese cloth) pasted on with Plaster of Paris mixed with a little dextrine or glue size can be used for one of your layers. At least nine coats should be used to build up a satisfactory thickness, and more layers if the model is large. See that the paper is pressed well down, smooth out creases and avoid air bubbles by checking each layer as it is completed. The thickness can be tested by plunging a hat pin through. Care should be taken to see that edges are not overlapping the mould. If they are, it will be hard to remove when dry. Teachers should make sure at this stage that children's works are named, as all the models look alike. Many arguments can be avoided if this is done! Models should be allowed to dry.

Fig. 10 Placing strips over a plate mould. Notice that the print on each strip is following the same direction on this layer. The second one will go across in the opposite way. This helps you to count the layers and get an even thickness. The plate has been greased so that the paper will not stick to it. A bowl facilitates the dipping of strips into the paste. The newspaper has been torn vertically with the grain of the paper, so that straight pieces have been obtained

When the object is nearly dry – this can take from four hours to forty, as it depends on the warmth of the room – trim the edges with sharp scissors. The mould should come away easily when the papier maché is dry. Some outside papers may loosen, and should be pasted down. If sticking does occur, a blunt knife can be used to prise the model gently from the mould. The rim should now be neatened and strengthened. This is done by pasting small strips of paper over the edge, as shown in fig. 12.

The surface can be smoothed by rubbing carefully with fine sandpaper.

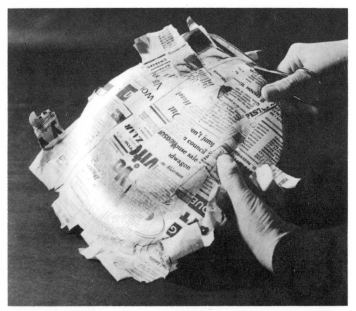

Fig. 11   Trimming the plate edges with scissors before removing from the mould. If this is not possible, for instance when using a plastic bowl which has a fold over the top, draw a chalk line round before moving from the mould. It is then easy to get it even, as measurements can be taken from the top

Decorating

Before decorating, an all-over layer of colour or gesso should be applied, as this will cover the printed surface and seal it. Sometimes two coats may be necessary, sandpapering the first one before applying the second. This provides a smooth base onto which paint can be put easily. It is a good idea to plan your designs on paper first. A source of inspiration may be needed; look through books showing examples of pattern work on pottery or papier maché. South American and primitive art show particularly the interesting effects that can be obtained by limiting the number of colours used. Museums often have in their collections wonderful specimens of applied pattern.

Those who can draw can make a sketch book and look at the many wonderful designs there are around them. Fruit, both whole or sliced, can stimulate and give one ideas — vegetables, flowers, wood grain and many other natural forms inspire designs.

Doodles, on the blotter, in the telephone directory or wherever, are another starting point for patterns.

Geometric designs are usually successful. To paint these a steady hand is required, and great care; but one has only to look at early Greek pottery to see how effective such designs are. This type of pattern can also be obtained by cutting squares, circles and other mathematical shapes from coloured papers and applying them as collage.

When decoration has been completed, the objects should be made waterproof with varnish, polish or lacquer.

Fig. 12   The diagram shows how the edges of the plate are neatened by small strips. In order to preserve the uniform thickness and avoid bumps, butt the edges together as closely as possible. Do not overlap

Fig. 13 *Plate* by Betty Lorrimar. This was carried out by the mould method and, after tidying the edges, it was decorated with geometric shapes. The colours used were to match the décor of the room in which it was to be displayed

Fig. 14 *Bowl* by Gillian Ward, aged 11. Modelled over a plastic bowl. Gillian looked at examples of primitive art before painting. She limited her colours to white, brown and black

Some people feel that making models from moulds is not as creative as making freely-formed shapes. This may be so if rigid copying of design follows. However, having based a satisfying shape on another, if exciting patterns and decorating methods are used, a completely fresh object emerges. In pottery making without a wheel moulds are frequently used, but the resulting articles are not necessarily stereotyped. A mould is really a practical aid and it is often a great help when modelling. There are great advantages in the method, for instance a whole set of decorative plates could be made. Reasonably even shapes are obviously useful for this.

Moulds are also helpful when making objects requiring a good curved shape—flower petals, tops of hats and other similar models. Masks are much easier and quicker to make with a mould of some kind to form the basic shape.

Fig. 15 *Bowl* by Betty Lorrimar. Also modelled over a plastic bowl. About six layers of papier maché were used. It was painted with poster colours and then coated with clear matt varnish

Making maracas

A simple and effective object to make using the mould method is a rhythm instrument or rattle. An old electric light bulb is needed. These come in various shapes and sizes, the larger ones are best.

Small strips of paper are torn. These are dipped into a bowl of paste (fig. 16) and applied evenly over the whole bulb. About six layers are needed. When dry and hard the bulb is banged onto a hard surface (fig. 17). This should break the glass inside and will give a rattle noise when shaken.

Decoration can be put on, and an attractive maraca is the result.

Numerous items can be made by moulding — decorative plates and bowls, vases for artificial flowers, and trays, for instance. A vase for real flowers is made by putting papier maché over a jam or honey jar. In this instance the jar is not removed.

Fig. 16

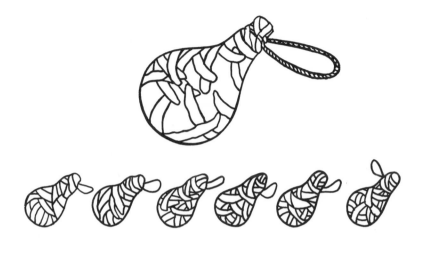

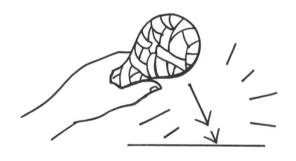

Fig. 17

Making trays

A tray made of papier maché is very light and strong, as well as attractive. There are two methods of making trays, both easy. One is by moulding. By using this method, you obtain a replica of another tray. A more creative way is to use a cardboard pattern as a base and work over it. This gives great freedom, as you can plan the size and shape of tray that you need. Old grocery cartons or shirt boxes can also provide the basis of a tray. They just need to be cut down, leaving sides the height you require. Holes for handles are made at both ends. Several layers of pasted paper are then applied over the whole surface.

Many trays made in the eighteenth century were painted by eminent artists, see fig. 20. These are very beautiful, but simple, colourful designs are also effective and may be painted or put on with découpage.

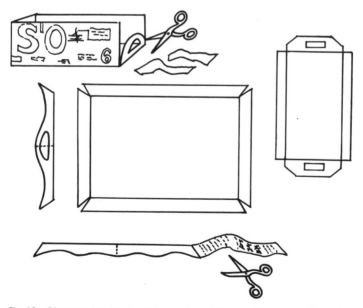

Fig. 18 Diagrams showing simple tray patterns. It is a good idea to cut this out in corrugated cardboard, as this does not warp when the layers of pasted paper are applied. Note paper templates for obtaining curved sides

Fig. 19 *Tray* by Margaret Hickson. A useful tray made from the pattern shown in fig. 18. It was decorated with two layers of black tissue paper followed by a cut-out shape in fluorescent display paper. It is modern and effective

Fig. 20 This tray, in complete contrast to the one above, was made in the middle of the nineteenth century by B. Walton and Company of Birmingham. The painting shows a warranted Crusader's castle. It is delicate and beautiful, in the style of the period. Victoria and Albert Museum, London

Bottle figures

To make these, bottles of any shape or size may be used. They can remain upright or be used horizontally. The shapes or positions help to suggest the sort of characters or animals to make. Plastic containers are particularly suitable, especially if children are working on them. They are light, unbreakable and parts may be cut to help the modelling, see fig. 25.

The first stage is to cover the whole surface — including the bottom — with two or three layers of torn newspaper strips which have been dipped in paste. This is so that if the model is dropped at a later stage and the glass is broken, it will not come through.

Fig. 21 *Bottle figure* by Margaret Hickson. This lady makes an unusual decoration. She was first painted all over in tan poster colour. Her hair is from a theatrical make-up box. The small water jar on her head is, of course, papier maché. The use of net and sequins help to give her the authentic air of eastern mystery

Fig. 22 The bottle covered all over with pasted newspaper. The head is crumpled paper attached to the bottle with strips

Pastey, crumpled paper is added to the top, in order to build up a head. It is attached to the figure by using long strips of newsprint.

Arms are made by rolling tubes of pasted paper and attaching them to the body with more pasted strips (fig. 23).

Fig. 23 The arms being added by using strips to fix them to the body

To make a horizontal animal you must place tubes over the bottle as shown in fig. 24. The model should be left on its back until the legs dry and harden so that they can take the weight of the bottle. The leg tubes are made stronger by using very tightly rolled tubes, or by inserting a thin piece of wire before rolling the paper.

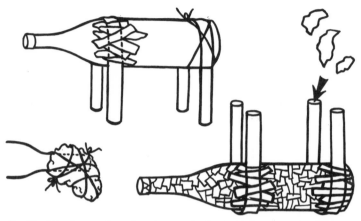

Fig. 24   This diagram shows how legs can be fixed without using wire. The two tubes are tied over the bottle and then stuffed with paper pieces. Paper strips are then pasted over to hold them in position. In the bottom left the crumpled paper is tied to begin the forming of the head

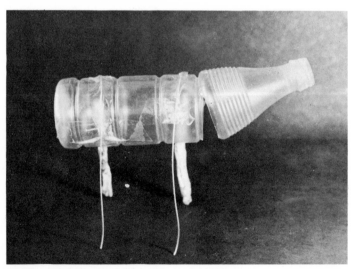

Fig. 25   A plastic bottle which is to be used for a horse. Wire has been curved over the back to form legs. It is held in place with gummed tape. The bottle neck has been cut half way, so that it may be bent upwards

Further modelling can be applied by crumpling pastey paper. It must be fixed to the object with strips, as shown in fig. 24.

When dry the surface should be checked and made as smooth as possible by applying small pieces of pasted paper over bad joins or holes.

Left
Fig. 26   *Lady with her basket* by Linda Steel, aged 12. A figure showing imaginative use of materials. The basket is made of hemp and lined with paper; there is a good combination of textures and pattern

Right
Fig. 27   *Bottle figure* by Margaret Hickson. The gay hula girl was painted first in chocolate brown poster colour. Her hair was then added — black, unravelled wool (yarn). Some odd bits of raffia were used to make her skirt. She has gold bracelets of curtain rings, a necklet of small shells and tiny fruit from an old hat trimming were used to make her earrings. Her flowers are coloured tissue paper

Fig. 28 *Drummer* by Pasqua Jackson, aged 11. A bottle was used for the horse. The figure is based on paper tubes

Fig. 29 *Guitar player* by Jennifer Prance, aged 13

Decoration

When dry and hard, decoration can proceed. A good scrap box is essential at this point, so that plenty of scope can be given for the imaginative use of materials. Hair can be glued on — string, raffia, wool (yarn), fur, feathers, cotton wool (absorbent cotton), are all suitable for this.

The horseguard in fig. 30 has armour made from kitchen foil. His helmet is of silver paper. The sword is a piece of wire.

It is amazing the ingenious ideas that evolve when making these little figures. Great fun can be had with very simple means.

Fig. 30 *Guardsman*. Bottle figure by Pasqua Jackson, aged 11. The soldier figure is made from papier-maché tubes with wire inserted. The horse is a horizontal bottle

Toys

Papier maché has long been used to make toys. It is an easy material to work with. In the nineteenth century delightful automatic toys were made. Musical box figures were most attractive. Monkeys were particularly popular and were made to perform amazing feats, such as puffing cigarettes and dancing. They were also made in groups and formed small orchestras playing simple percussion instruments. Simpler toys were made too, the cow in fig. 32 is an example. It was made for a small child to pull along. Other attractive subjects were decorated Easter Eggs, schoolroom globes, dolls and the traditional Jack-in-the-Box.

German toymakers were prominent in the use of papier maché. Toy soldiers were made in the early nineteenth century both in France and in Germany. They declined in popularity because they had to be larger than those made of wood or lead. In America, Ludwig Greiner of Philadelphia was famous for his papier-maché dolls. In England other pulp compositions were made, sawdust being added to make a stronger substance.

More recent examples of papier-maché toys are to be found in Mexico, India, China and Japan. Toy animals and dolls are the most popular subjects. They are painted in gay patterns and colours. The home toymaker today can be inspired by these models from the past, and invent and create new ones. Children are quite capable of making interesting playthings for themselves. The Noah's Ark in fig. 104 is an example of this; and other subjects suggest themselves — dolls' houses and all the accessories, farms with animals, zoos, the old woman who lived in a shoe, shops and their wares, and many more. An old grocery carton, some pulp papier maché and a few paints are the only materials needed to provide hours of interest.

Fig. 31   Music box figure; automaton. French, *c.* 1880. Museum of Childhood, Edinburgh

Fig. 32   Cow, Thuringian toy, *c.* 1870. This lovely study of a cow can be pulled along. As it moves, the bell attached to its collar will ring. Museum of Childhood, Edinburgh

Fig. 31

Fig. 32

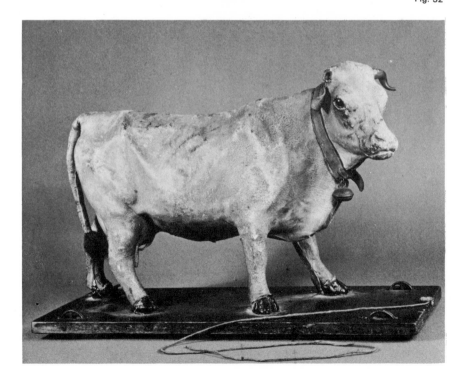

Small figures and animals

All types of figures can be made, very static or showing movement.

Newspaper sheets are rolled into tubes with thin wire inside for easy bending, to form shapes of bodies, legs and arms. These are tied at the ends with wool (yarn), string or paper tape.

The various pieces are joined together – using string again – and should be made to form the shape of the figure required.

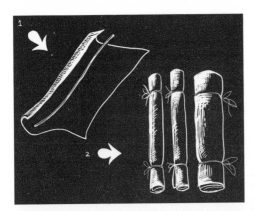

Fig. 33   The newspaper sheet is rolled round the wire and tied. The narrow shapes will form arms or legs, or both. The wider tube will be for the body

Fig. 34   The pieces are joined together to form either a human figure or an animal. The inserted wire enables the model to be bent into any position

Strips of well-pasted newsprint are now 'bandaged' over it. It is often easier at this stage to nail an upright figure onto a small wooden stand. It may need to be propped until it is dry — hard Plasticine is useful for this. When mounted on a platform the figures are easier to model at the next stage.

When the models are firm, further modelling with crumpled pastey paper can be done, but make sure plenty of strips are used to secure shapes. Also support if necessary, as models are heavy when wet. Drying must again take place. When they are firm and hard, tidying can proceed. Obviously if the face is full of cracks and creases it will be difficult to paint. Small pieces of newspaper can be pasted over any such faults.

Models are then ready for the exciting task of decorating, either with paint or with applied materials. You will see by the

Fig. 35 Whether animal or human, the model is built to the required shape. Crumpled, pastey paper is used to form the heads or other features. It is fixed by gummed tape (not the cellulose kind, as it will not stick to damp or wet paper). Paper strips can be used if no tape is available. The original tube is indicated by the dotted line in the diagram. The ears — top left — diagram — are added

photographs some of the interesting results that can be realized.

Small figures are absorbing subjects to make in papier maché. They stimulate the imagination and lead to the most ingenious use of materials. They encourage observation and awareness of so

Fig. 36 *Beggar* by Jacqueline Creffield, aged 12. A charming figure, as it shows such a good combination of textures. The natural hessian used for his coat, the small scale check pattern for his trousers, blend well. He carries a small sack to hold his few belongings

many things that would otherwise be ignored. There is the toffee paper (candy wrapper) that could become a flower, the tinfoil lid which could make a shield or tray, small beads, old rope or woollens to be unravelled — the possibilities are endless!

Fig. 37 *Artist* by Manda Bray, aged 12. He paints boldly on his easel picture. His rather unkempt hair is of hemp. The check scarf and striped overall are both correct in scale. The trousers are made of hessian (burlap). The palette is cardboard. The wire foundation helped to bend him into his painter's pose

Fig. 38 *Horse* by Jane Slidders, aged 12. After the first stage in modelling, the horse was fixed to the wooden base with a few small nails. More modelling was added. When dry it was covered with small pieces of natural coloured hessian. This gives a pleasing texture. Hemp was used for the mane and tail. The face was painted with poster colour. The wooden stand is painted and has sand glued to it in places

Fig. 39 *Horse and carriage* by Melanie Brett-Smith, aged 12 years. A pleasant group. The lady in her Sunday clothes is perhaps on her way to church. Her little dog – cotton wool (absorbent cotton) over the newspaper base – is accompanying her. The 'finish' is not perfect, but this is more than made up for in its interest and charm

Fig. 40 *Native figure* by Judy Taylor, aged 12. Four paper tubes form the basis of this figure. They are covered with a layer of pasted pieces. It is decorated with poster colours in a straightforward manner. There are no collage additions

Fig. 41 *Skier* by Elizabeth Temple-Murray, aged 11. A piece of plywood was used as a base. Pastey, crumpled newspaper was placed at one end to represent the ski run. The whole was covered with a sheet of paper to give a smooth effect. The figure was built up from tubes of news-paper, the head being crumpled paper with small pieces pasted over. The clothes were made from old woolly bits and were glued and sewn on

Fig. 42 *Owl* by Margaret Hickson. The preliminary modelling was done with crumpled, pasted paper. The beak and shaping were formed when this was dry and hard. An old pillow was raided for feathers and these were carefully glued on — light brown in front, dark brown sides and head, light grey around the face. A branch was found and the owl fixed on by its papier-maché covered wire feet. These had been inserted into the body while it was still soft. The eyes were bought from a craft supply shop. The ferns around the lower part of the branch had been pressed before use

Free, loose paper modelling

The owl and the cat were both modelled freely with pasted, crumpled paper. This is a quick and creative method. The paper is dipped into a bowl of paste and the basic shape is loosly formed. Paper strips are then put over to hold the shape, and it is allowed to dry. String can also be used to hold the modelling in position. When dry the basic core can be added to, and the final shape evolved. Guard against squeezing the crumpled paper too tightly at the first stage. If this is done the technique changes, and pulp modelling becomes necessary. Expect the model, in the primary stage, to look rather un-formed. The aim is to have a foundation for further modelling. Sometimes this beginning flops a little or bends in a certain direction and suggests the pose to follow.

The cat, fig. 43, leans slightly to one side, and this was because the preliminary forming dried in that direction. It did make the cat more perky.

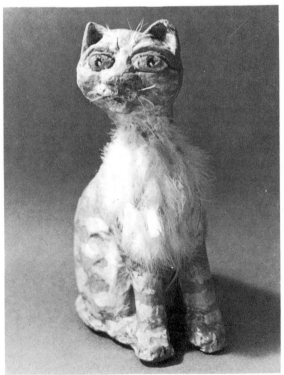

Fig. 43 *Cat* by Betty Lorrimar. Freely formed from pasted paper. The front paws are from two paper tubes, which were added at the second stage. The whiskers and white chest are made from feathers which were put on after the cat had been painted and varnished

Large figures

These are ideal subjects for group work, although figures can be made on one's own without much effort.

It saves time to make a framework of chicken wire. This also makes the final figure firm. However wire is difficult for young children to manipulate, so that it may be preferable to use one of the other methods.

The frame can be built in the same way as is done when making smaller models. Obviously the rolls of newspaper must be bigger, and the centre core well padded. A quicker method is to stuff a thin sack with paper to make a body, stuff paper into old stockings for arms and legs, and stuff a paper bag for the head.

When the basic shape has been formed, it is covered with layers of pasted paper. At least three layers are advisable, and plenty of paste should be used so that the model will dry hard.

Fig. 44 The preliminary stage when making a large, free-standing woman figure. The lower part is papier maché over cardboard. The inside is hollow. This type of model stands easily and is light to move

Fig. 45 *King Charles* by Susan Brown, aged 14. This character was modelled over a wire frame. The newspaper was pasted and wrapped around. Little painting was done on this figure. His face was covered with an old thick stocking, as were his hands. Eyes and mouth were painted on the stocking cover. His hair is of wood shavings, which have a natural curl. He is life-size and makes an amusing subject. He is holding a papier mâché goblet, and has obviously imbibed the wine it contained!

When the framework is dry, the final modelling can be applied. This is done with the crumpled paper and strips method.

The figures can be painted or clothed. Smoothness cannot be obtained so easily when working on a large scale, but the rougher texture has its own charm. A gesso can be brushed over of course, which does give a smoother effect.

Amusing and decorative figures can be made, and given real chairs to sit on. They are effective in displays and exhibitions, and make attractive party decorations too. More patience is obviously required, but once the models are under way interest is maintained. It is much more interesting to work on figures of this kind if there is a purpose in view. The group of characters opposite are an example of this (fig. 47).

Fig. 46 *Spanish lady* by Susan Agnew, aged 14. This was began in the same way as shown in figure 44, with a card-board form for the lower half. Her dress was made-up from pieces of material found in an old theatrical dress basket. The face was painted with poster col-ours. Her mantilla is covered cardboard. The flower is tissue paper on thin wire

Fig. 47　A group of figures made for a project designed to attract attention and to inform the public of the help they can receive from the social services. The aim was to represent a typical family group. The figures were built up gradually over a core of rolled paper tubes. The clothing is all of newspaper which was dipped into paste and modelled onto the figures. Everthing is made of paper except the chair. They were painted with poster colours. Made by sixth-form girls at Maidenhead High School (aged 16)

Figs 48 and 49 *Lion* by Sheila Buxton and Isla Cameron, aged 14. Animals can also be made on a large scale. This friendly lion was modelled over big cardboard cylinders, so that his centre core is hollow. This was done both for speed and to keep him light and easily moveable. He is painted with poster colours, and the mane and tail end are of hemp

Above Lion – front view. Here you see his gentle expression and pleasant personality

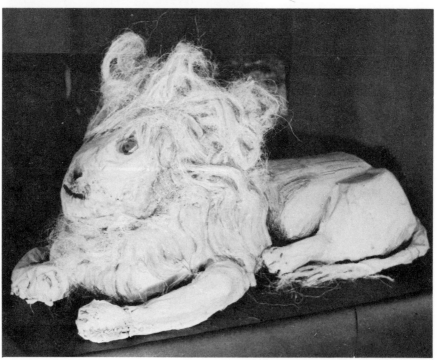

Fig. 50   Modern advertising. Photograph by Goran Bjorling of papier-maché head,
S. Vea Agency, Stockholm

How to make paper pulp

At this stage another modelling process can be considered — paper pulp. This can be used like clay, but remember to allow for shrinkage — features should be bold.

Tear small pieces of newspaper and soak in water overnight (fig. 51). Drain off surplus water and beat the mixture with a stick, rolling pin or similar object (fig. 52). You can also squeeze and rub the mixture with your hands.

Paste (roughly one-third paste to paper pulp) and a little whitening can now be added. It should be stirred in well.

Another method is to soak papier-maché egg cartons overnight. They are then beaten in the same way and will make a pliable pulp when paste is added.

Never cut the paper when making pulp, as the hard edges take longer to break down.

If a fine mixture is required for modelling small things, paper tissues may be used instead of newspaper. A quick way of breaking down the paper fibres is to boil the mixture instead of soaking overnight. Any large pan or metal pail is suitable for this. Boil slowly and do not allow the pan to burn dry. An occasional stir will help. The pulp will still need beating when cool.

An electric blender would help to make a smoother consistency of course, but that will only be considered by the really keen enthusiast!

If the pulp is not to be used immediately it must be kept damp. A wet cloth laid over the bowl is usually sufficient to do this, otherwise the mixture can be placed into a plastic bag and tied so that it is airtight.

The advantage of using pulp for modelling is that small objects can be completed in one session without waiting for drying. This is useful when young children are trying out the craft. For larger sculptures a section at a time should be completed, as the papier maché is very heavy when it is wet, and shapes may become distorted. Armatures can be used, as with clay modelling. When dry and hard, models can be rubbed down smooth with sandpaper before painting or finishing.

Sculpture

Making serious sculpture from papier maché is becoming increasingly popular. Papier maché has always been used to make constructions in window displays, and this has led modern artists to consider it useful and versatile for serious compositions. It is such a flexible material that free expression is possible.

Some sculptors use the papier maché as a base for their work and superimpose other materials. Others use it in combination with these, and the papier maché can be seen. Unfortunately the substance cannot be left outside unless properly treated with many layers of lacquer. Papier maché can be made durable, as is attested by the fact that it was used in the nineteenth century for coach building, ships' cabins and other outdoor objects. However it is not recommended for outside sculpture. For indoor models it is an excellent medium. The use of colour in sculpture, long neglected, is now becoming popular. Patterns and colours are easily painted onto papier maché, and any type of paint may be used. Size need not be limited. As the material is light it can be moved around to different parts of the room or building without trouble. The worry of whether the floor can stand the weight does not arise, which is useful for flat dwellers!

Any shape can be evolved, so the sculptor is not restricted in expressing ideas.

Left
Fig.53　American Treasury figure – 5,000 dollars in pulped bills! The head is meant to be George Washington. It is not too well moulded. Museum of Childhood, Edinburgh

Right
Fig. 54　American Valentine toy. Clown, 'Aelian' or won't-lie-down figure, *c.* 1900. Museum of Childhood, Edinburgh

Fig. 55　Mechanical elephant. French, *c.* 1880. Museum of Childhood, Edinburgh

Fig. 56 *The Thing* by Niki de Saint-Phalle, 1963. A sculpture in various materials including papier maché. Height 72 ins (183 cms). Photo Hanover Gallery, London

56 CREATIVE PAPIER MACHE

Models can be made by using paper pulp to create a solid shape or figure. Size will be according to the amount of patience you have! Models can be quite gigantic, as long as they are built in stages — as with clay — otherwise the weight of the material when wet presses the lower part out of shape.

Another way is by creating a basic figure with wire and then covering with pasted sheets of paper. If a large frame is made it is a good idea to cover the wire by binding with strips of old rag. This stops the paper from slipping when it is applied.

Models can be rubbed down when dry and then painted. If a rough, attractive final surface is required, sand mixed with water-glass (sodium silicate) can be applied with a palette knife — or any flexible flat tool.

Plaster-coated bandages also provide a pleasing effect. These can be obtained from model makers' shops, and are very easy to apply.

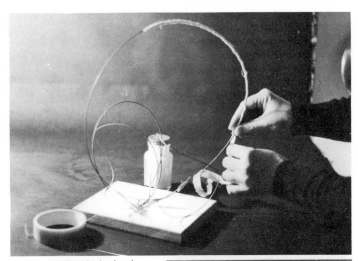

Fig. 57 Binding the basic wire frame with cotton strips

Fig. 58 The halfway stage. Parts of the model built-up with newspaper dipped in paste

Plaster-coated bandages are very useful when making lively small figures and sculpture. A wire frame is easily covered, and the result is most attractive, with no other finish required. It is rather expensive to buy ready for use, but worth having. It is mainly used by people making model railways and similar things, as it can be put over shapes used in landscapes. If it is hard to obtain, ordinary bandage can be dipped into wet plaster to produce more or less the same effect, but home-made efforts often

Fig. 59 *Ballet dancer* by Karen Bunce, aged 12. A wire figure was constructed and bent to show movement. This was then nailed to a small wooden base. Papier-maché strips were applied loosely over the frame and left to dry. The final surface is of plaster impregnated binding, which is obtainable at most craftwork suppliers

crumble when dry. The ready-prepared kind does not do this.

Papier-maché sculpture models, such as the one above, are very striking in appearance. Some of the wire framework has hardly been covered. This provides a good contrast with the solidly filled areas. String or wire lines are effective used in combination with papier-maché formed shapes. Glass or plastic can also be used to enrich the surface. There are, in fact, endless possibilities worth exploring in this versatile medium.

Fig. 60 *Sculpture* by Gillian Griffith, aged 17. Built over a wire frame which was fixed by nails to a wooden base. Rag was wound round the frame before strips of pasted paper were applied. It is painted in poster colours

Masks

Before beginning, it is a good idea to look at examples of African, Chinese and Indian masks. These are usually bold in design and highly decorative. The ones shown here from the Pitt Rivers Museum, Oxford, are not of papier maché. Many native masks are carved, but some are modelled in pith, which is a pulped matter similar in consistency to papier-maché pulp. All are interesting, and provide useful ideas for design. The carved wooden one on the left shows how effective the sloping mouth is and how expressive it can be. The other features are boldly shown too. The other mask shows exaggerated forms, and these are further enhanced by the use of hair and painted decoration. Such masks were used in ceremonial dances and religious rites. Today they are admired for their artistic qualities and they have inspired many modern designers.

Left
Fig. 61   Carved wooden mask. Pitt Rivers Museum, Oxford

Right
Fig. 62   Mask, Ceylon, painted and with added collage. Pitt Rivers Museum, Oxford

There are several ways of creating masks and the following are the simplest methods.

Find a pail lid, large plate, bin (garbage can) lid, or something similar, for use as a base. Cover over with a layer of wet paper — the outer side of the lid, plate etc. is best. Onto this paste about six layers of newspaper. Crumple up pasted paper and model the nose, eyebrows, and other features. Fix them into position with paper strips.

Animal noses, which need to be larger, can be made by using parts of cardboard tubes or boxes. These are covered with papier maché and joined to the head with paper strips.

A wire frame can be used instead of a box to build up large shapes, as this will make the mask lighter if it is to be worn for dramatic productions. This is not important if decoration is the

Fig. 63 *Mask* by Marion Simmonds, aged 11. This amusing horse was made without using a frame. It was built up on the back of a large plate. The nose was crumpled paper with strips round to hold it together

Fig. 64

Fig. 65

purpose. If such a frame is used it is made first, and then linked to the modelling on the mould with paper strips. It is easily joined to the base and will be quite firm when dry.

Another way to make a successful head is to model first in clay or Plasticine. If the mask is to be worn, remember to curve the face. Model in an exaggerated way, so that forms will not be lost when the newspaper is put over. Before doing this a layer of wet tissue paper should be put over the clay. You will find that this goes over the forms easily and can be pressed carefully into dents in the modelling.

Next put on about six layers of pasted paper. Use small pieces for the detailed modelling, larger on cheeks or big surfaces. Care must be taken to see that the modelled forms do not disappear. When dry the mask can be removed from the mould. If there are any weak pieces they can be patched with pasted paper on the back of the model. The edges can be tidied in the same way as when making plates (page 22).

Other ways of making masks are equally simple. A balloon can be inflated and a model made onto it. If more than a face is required this is a very useful method. The balloon can be blown up to the size needed. When the papier maché is dry the balloon is pricked and is then easily removed.

Paper picnic plates can also be used as bases for masks, and these can remain as part of the finished creation, so that a strong, firm result is obtained.

Large paper bags make suitable bases too, especially when made of coarse brown paper.

Masks can be painted when the modelling is complete. Accessories may also be added. A wide variety of materials can be used for hair; and sequins and jewels give exciting results. Patterns can be freely added.

Masks make unusual wall decorations and are also useful for parties or dramatic productions. The illustrations give an idea of the variety of effects which are obtainable (figs 63–5).

Fig. 64 *Mask* by Ann Waring, aged 11. This mask was modelled over a bin (garbage can) lid. It is probably effective because it has been stated so simply. The prominent eyes and nose are dominating, and the uneven teeth give an air of amusement

Fig. 65 *Horse mask* by Kay Bradley, aged 12. Modelled over the outside of a plastic bowl, the form was freely formed with paper which had been dipped into paste

Puppets

Children love to make puppets and act with them. They are quite simple to make.

Roll a paper tube so that it is large enough for one or two fingers to be inserted into it. It can be stuck with brown gummed paper. This acts as a neck and the central pillar of the head. Pulp papier maché is modelled on the top part. This should be quite roughly done, without worrying yet about the final shape. It is then laid to dry. When hard, modelling can really begin. The solid core will give firm support and the human head or animal can be formed. Model boldly — this allows for shrinkage and also for the exaggeration which is necessary in theatre design.

When dry, the surface can be smoothed with sandpaper before painting.

Tackle the painting in a clear bold way, so that the expression and design reads from a distance. If the head is for a human character, hair can be added next. A variety of materials are suitable for this. Frayed jute is effective, as is raffia or string. Old woollen sweaters can be unthreaded — these give lovely curly

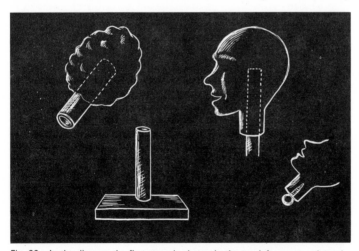

Fig. 66 In the diagram the first stage is shown in the top left corner — the pulp papier maché put onto a paper tube. Below this is a simple stand which is useful for putting the puppet head on to dry, model and paint. It is easily made, a piece of dowel is screwed or fitted into a wooden base. A firm tin lid with a nail hammered through can also be used. The head shown top right is fully formed. The lower right shows a screw inserted into the neck if a marionette is to be made. The neck in this case would have been stuffed with papier maché and be solid

hair effects. Fur and feathers can also be useful. Hands may be of material — felt is often used, as it does not fray. They can be modelled in papier maché too. This is done in the same way as when making the head — that is, onto paper tubes. These are smaller, as only one finger is used to work them, and shorter.

The dress is made, and care should be taken to see that the neck is not too wide and the sleeves are not too long.

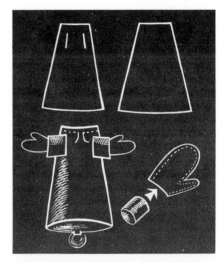

Fig. 67 The glove (hand) puppet dress pattern. Note that the back is slightly wider than the front, to allow for the bend of the hand. The two slits in the front piece are for inserting the sleeve and hand. The hands are easier to manipulate if a small paper tube is inserted at the wrist. The ring attached to the bottom of the completed dress is for hanging-up the puppet when not in use

Fig. 68 Three glove (hand) puppets by Alison Beattie, Karen Boyd, Joy Crockford, all aged 12. They were part of the cast of *Cinderella*

When this is completed the parts are sewn or glued together.

Another way to make a puppet head is to model first in Plasticine. Do not forget to include the neck when modelling. The head and neck are then covered with a layer of wet tissue paper. This goes well into deeper sections of the modelling. About six layers of small pieces of pasted newsprint are then put over. When dry the head is cut in half, so that the Plasticine can be extracted. Small amounts may be left to strengthen the nose, ears, etc. The two parts are joined again with paper strips. It is important when making puppet heads in this way to put the correct number of layers over the preliminary model. If this is not done it is very difficult to join the two parts at the later stage. The early modelling must also be exaggerated, as much of it is lost in the covering process. This type of head is lighter when completed, as it is hollow; thus it is suitable for glove (hand) puppets.

A puppet head can also be made simply by crumpling up pasted paper into a shape. This core is covered with strips and left to dry. Modelling is then added as before.

Marionettes can be made in papier maché. The pulp method is best for this, as the solid material can have screws inserted to join the several parts, or you can work over thin pieces of wood. The neck need not be a tube but needs to be modelled so that the dress can be attached to it.

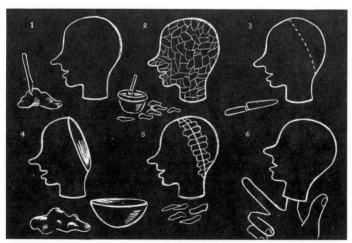

Fig. 69   A diagram to show stages in modelling a puppet head in Plasticine: 1 the model with modelling material and tool nearby; 2 the head covered with layers of paper and paste; 3 when dry the head is cut where shown; 4 the Plasticine is extracted; 5 the head is joined again with paper strips; 6 model ready for decorating

Scenery and stage properties

As a material for making stage properties papier maché is very useful. Imitation fruit, meat and similar things can be made by the pulp-modelling technique. They can be thrown around the stage safely as they are unbreakable. Bowls, pottery, tankards, shields and a host of other objects can be made by using the mould method. Again they have the advantage of being unbreakable.

Rocks can be built over a wire framework and can be made solid enough for sitting on and yet light to move — an important point for stage work. Many exciting television and film sets make use of papier maché. In fig. 71 you can see stage flats decorated by using the tones obtained in newspaper photographs to make designs and pictures.

The flats themselves are made from papier maché. A wooden frame is covered with pasted newspaper sheets. Care must be taken to see that both sides are evenly coated, so the flat will dry without warping. When hard and dry it can be decorated with paint or collage. Flats made in this way are very light and easy to move, very cheap to produce and any size or shape is obtainable. Smaller boards for stagework, or even lightweight drawing boards, can be made by pasting sheets of newspaper together and laying them between boards or metal sheets to dry. They can be sawn to shape and painted or varnished when hard.

Fig. 70 *Hand mirror* by Margaret Hickson. Odd pieces of mirror glass need not be discarded. Here is one inserted into papier maché. It is light to hold, and interesting in shape. Decoration on the surround can match your décor. This type of mirror is also useful for stage work

Fig. 71 These stage flats were used with matching ones to build up a room for a scene in the opera *The Bartered Bride*. The idea was to suggest folk decoration in a modern idiom. The patterns were not painted but are in collage. Different tones obtained from pictures in newspapers were used. A pleasing texture resulted, and the monochrome background achieved enhanced the colourful costumes of the actors

Fig. 72 *Mask* by Karen Norris, Jacqueline Palfrey, Anna Reid, all aged 13

Fig. 73 *Black cat* by Victoria Fox, aged 13

Fig. 74

Fig. 75

Decorative flowers

These are particularly attractive and useful in the winter, when fresh flowers are scarce. They provide colourful and unusual party decorations.

Wire is used to make the stems. First place a piece of wire onto a piece of pasted paper and roll it to enclose the wire. Strips of paper are then put over this, using plenty of paste, to make a first stem.

The flower heads can be made in various ways. They may be shaped with wire and then have paper strips applied over them. They can be made from thin sheets of papier maché, which is easily cut into shapes. Pulp paper can be used to form more solid forms. Moulds also provide a number of flower-like shapes — the bottom of a basin for large ones, the lower part of a bottle or glass tumbler, the back of a spoon, and many other objects.

When the shapes have been evolved, the wire stems are carefully poked through a hole made in the base of the flower with a needle or compass point. The wire is then bent over to hold the head in position. A little papier maché can be used to fix it firmly, so that it does not slip. This is done before decoration is applied.

If newspaper has been used, paint or collage or a mixture of the two can be used to decorate. Patterns may be put on, but interesting effects are often achieved by using varied types of collage. Rice, sequins, dried peas, lentils and similar items can be stuck on with strong clear glue. An attractive result is achieved by using coloured tissue papers instead of newspaper. There are exotic colours available. This does not need to be painted, of course, but added collage does give textural interest. Do not overdo this, or the beauty of the tissue paper is lost. To increase transparency and bring out colour to the full, varnish can be applied. Make sure the paste is really dry before doing this.

When completed the flowers can be displayed in a papier maché vase.

Fig. 74 *Candelabra* by Margaret Hickson. Papier-maché tubes were placed spontaneously into a base of crumpled papier-maché sheets. Small pieces of copper tube are inserted into the tops, so that the candles are firmly held. The model was decorated with fireproof paint as a precautionary measure

Fig. 75 *Decorative flowers* by Margaret Hickson. Painted in vivid colours, these forms are ideal for party decoration or stage decor

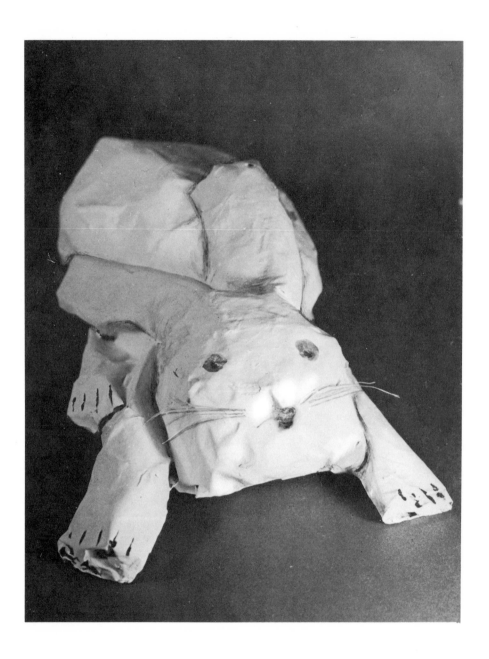

Fig. 76 *Rabbit* by Susan Boxer, aged 12. This was freely modelled with loosely, crumpled paper and paste. It was smoothed with a layer of small paper pieces and then painted in poster colours. It seems to catch the very essence of a rabbit

Jewellery

Using papier maché as a material for jewellery making gives one great scope. It can be free in shape and large and chunky, as it is light to wear. Another great advantage is that it can be unique if you make it yourself, and you can decorate it to match your outfit. It has been used by modern designers to create exciting and unusual effects which cannot be obtained by using more traditional methods. You can make whole sets to match one another — bracelets, beads and earrings. Before you begin, look at pictures of jewellery made by the ancient Egyptians, the Romans and other civilizations. You will find that they created some most exciting ornaments, which appear very modern in design. You will be stimulated and get ideas of unusual ways of shaping your jewellery. Another source of inspiration is to find pictures of really modern pieces — or visit a museum or exhibition. The Museum of Modern Art in New York has shown really unusual pieces of jewellery — made from baked bread, machinery, and of course, from papier maché.

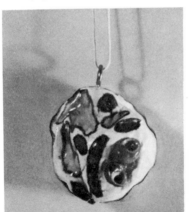

Left
Fig. 77 *Pendant* by Susan Lewarne, aged 13. A small amount of pulp was pressed into a free shape. Small niches were made which were later to hold beads. When dry a hole was made with a compass point for the neck cord to go through. The form was sandpapered before painting and glueing on beads. Varnish was finally applied

Right
Fig. 78 *Pendant* by Sarah Tilley, aged 13. A piece of moulded paper pulp was made. The ring used to attach it to the neck cord is a picture hanger (called passe partout ring in US), which was inserted when modelling. Painting was done in poster colours before varnishing. Beads had been glued on first

Ways of making beads

Beads can be made by putting layers of papier maché round a pencil, piece of dowelling or a similar thin tube. Grease the stick first, unless your first layer is of wet, unpasted paper. The thickness required will determine the number of layers you put on. When dry the thin, hard papier-maché tube is removed from the mould, and can be cut to varying sizes. The resulting beads are then painted, varnished and threaded. If wallpaper or coloured papers are used for the final layer, painting is not necessary. Ordinary beads often add a sparkle to the necklace if they are placed between the paper ones when threading.

Another way of making beads is to model shapes in pulp paper. Allow to dry and when hard rub with sandpaper or cover with a layer of tissue paper. Before painting make a hole in each bead so that they are ready to thread. This should be done with a compass point or strong needle.

Bracelets and earrings

Bracelets are made by rolling papier-maché tubes — as for bead making but larger, of course. Bottles or rolling pins can provide good moulds. When dry, the tube can be lightly sawn, or cut with a sharp knife, to provide several rings. They can be of various thicknesses. (Napkin rings are made in the same way.) Decoration can be applied with paint or collage. Raffia or wool (yarn) wound round the ring is often pleasing.

Pasted paper wound over a circle made of wire is another way of obtaining a bracelet. The advantage here is that you can make it to your own size without being tied to the diameter of a mould.

Earrings can be made as small rings or by the pulp method. Any shape can be evolved. It is better to buy the ear attachments from a craft shop or dealer in jewellery.

Pendants, brooches and rings

These can be modelled with paper pulp. When dry they may be painted and varnished. Pendants can be made attractive by adding collage, either on top of the paint or as part of the decoration. A strong glue should be used to add such things as sequins, small stones, materials, seeds and so on. The neck cord is threaded through a hole, which should be pierced through the pendant before decorating. This cord can be made from such things as shoe laces, string, plaited wool (braided yarn), chain, thin leather strips or copper wire.

As with beads, the colours and designs chosen can match your clothes; and you can wear the pendant knowing that you have a unique piece of jewellery.

Rings and brooches can also be made. It is possible to buy bases for these in most craft shops. When making a brooch you do not have to have a base, as the pin can be fixed to the back by using pasted strips and thus will be linked to the material when it is dry.

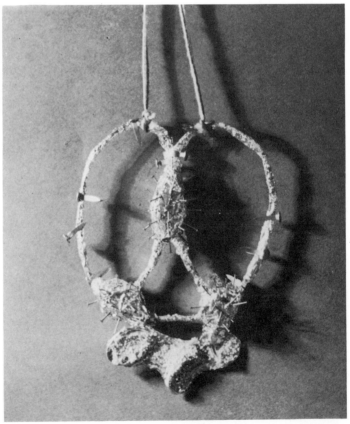

Fig. 79 *Necklet* by Wendy Chapman, aged 14. A wire framework was pasted over with a layer of paper strips. The heavier parts were made with pulp. Decoration was then applied — tiny brass nails were inserted, brass paper fasteners were spaced around the outside of the frame and small seeds were glued onto the base

Dolls

Dolls can be made completely of papier maché, as in the Mexican example in fig. 80, or just the head can be made with pulp papier maché. Papier-maché heads are much more attractive than the bought faces that are on sale in craft shops, and they are often more effective than material heads.

The head is modelled in the same way as when making a puppet (page 64). If a link is desired between the material of the body and the head, the papier-maché head can be covered with flesh-coloured stockinette and the features stitched instead of painted.

Costume dolls are made by using a cardboard base for the body and a solidly-modelled head. A whole series of these are an enjoyable project when studying the history of costume, or when designing for theatrical performances. This type of figure stands easily, as it has a cardboard base.

Fig. 80 Mexican doll. This is a grisly figure and is known as a 'death toy', c. 1930. Mexicans also make very gay brightly coloured dolls with similar construction. Museum of Childhood, Edinburgh

Fig. 81 *Doll* by Hilary Bevan, aged 13. Not the most beautiful of dolls, but it has its own personality. Her dress is made of rich brown velvet and so is her cap. She has a satin blouse and wears her best apron. String of a coarse type has made the little basket and provided the hair

Boxes

Boxes to your own size can be made and decorated in many ways. They are useful for keeping odds and ends of all kinds: jewellery, postage stamps and candies are just a few.

A piece of cardboard, either plain or corrugated, is used. The pattern (fig. 82) is drawn onto this and cut out. The lines which are to be folded are scored, to prevent their folding unevenly. Proportions are according to the requirements of the individual and the purpose of the box.

The sides are folded into position and held in place with pieces of sticky tape. The box is now covered with layers of pasted newspaper. The number used will depend on the size and strength needed, but at least three must be put over. The pieces may wrap over the outside and inside, so that the joints are strengthened. The final layer should include a strip that wraps round all four sides of the box. The box should be placed on a flat surface somewhere warm to dry. An airing cupboard is a good place, or a warm oven. To prevent warping the box can be tied round the sides with string or a rubber band.

The lid of the box should have weights placed on it to stop it from drying out of shape — a few stones will do. The lid may be fixed to the box using leather or material hinges, which are glued on when the parts are dry. If a loose lid is preferred, a small flange must be joined to the underside, so that it fits onto the box neatly. A strip of cardboard about half an inch wide is pasted into position with small strips of paper. More pieces are put on where necessary to make a good fit.

A small handle can be added. This may be a rolled piece of pasted newspaper or a modelled shape of paper pulp. The surface of the box can have papier maché relief decoration. Shells, beads or glass pieces inserted into this give an interesting effect. It may of course be painted, or découpage can be used. Beautiful examples exist from the eighteenth century (see fig. 83).

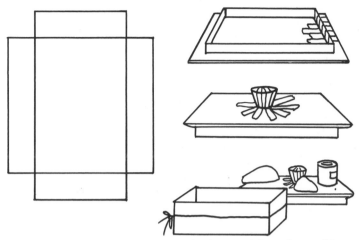

Fig. 82 Box pattern. Diagram to illustrate the pieces needed to make a small box, large boxes can of course be made in the same way and several boxes may be combined to make a unit. Also shown is the way to fix a flange on the lid.

Fig. 83 Writing box. Inlaid with mother-of-pearl and painted. Signed — Jennens and Betteridge, makers to the Queen. Nineteenth century. Victoria and Albert Museum, London

Hats and hat stands

For a lightweight hat that will protect you from sun, papier maché is an ideal material. There are several ways of making hats, and all methods are straightforward and easy. One style is obtained by using a balloon for a mould. It is blown up until the circumference is the same measurement as your head. Tie the balloon securely and then place it in a bowl which will hold it firmly while you work. Cover the top area to a depth of about ten inches with seven layers of pasted paper strips. Leave to dry. The resulting basic shape can now have any additions you wish. A brim is made by cutting the shape from a piece of layered papier maché. Add this to the top part with paper strips. When all the parts are firm and dry, puncture the balloon. The edges may now be trimmed with scissors. Bind round with paper strips to provide a neat finish – as with moulded plates. Test the hat for size. If it proves too large, more paper strips can be pasted inside. A coat of white emulsion paint should be applied. This is waterproof and is a good base for subsequent decoration. Acrylic or enamel paints are the best to use, as these are also waterproof, but if watercolour is preferred do not forget to cover with a good varnish or lacquer.

Another way of making a hat is to begin by pasting together about seven full size sheets of newspaper. Leave to dry on a flat surface. Next press them firmly with a hot iron to smooth out any creases. A hat pattern is now drawn onto the papier-maché sheet (fig. 84) – just the same as if you were using material. Cut out with scissors.

The headband is joined first with a strong glue, this forms the crown. The tip of the hat is inserted into this, again sticking with a strong glue. The brim is then added and fixed carefully to the lower part of the crown. A hat stand is useful, as the shape can be manipulated more easily. An iron is also a help. Edges should be neatened by applying small pasted strips all round.

Decoration can be bold and imaginative. A band may be put on to provide a better finish and hide the join if this shows. Paper flowers or bows may be added or the hat can be painted in an interesting way to match the outfit you will wear with it.

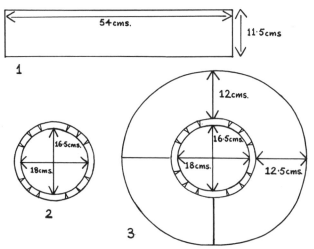

Fig. 84   Hat pattern. This shows the three main parts of the hat with average measurements: 1 the band which forms the crown of the hat; 2 the tip – the slash lines show where to cut so that it may be fixed easily to the head band; 3 the brim – again there are slash lines to enable the band to fit. The band is joined to make a circle – use white glue. Next fit tip of hat and finally join to the brim

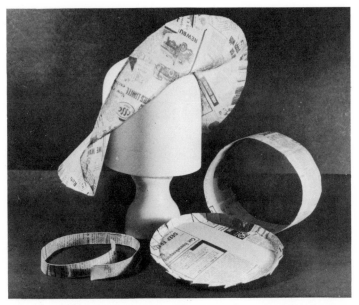

Fig. 85   The picture shows the parts of the hat ready for assembling. The wide brim is on the stand, the band is at the back and the tip is in front. Notice the cuts round the tip which enable it to be glued onto the band. The narrow curved strip on the left is the ribbon piece, which is placed over the join of brim and band

Fig. 86   The brim can be modelled to any shape when on the stand

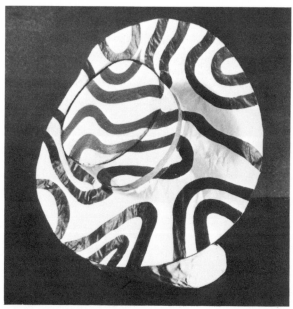

Fig. 87   *Completed hat* by Margaret Hickson. Back view. It has been painted in waterproof, acrylic colours — black and white with the ribbon piece red. It is both attractive and practical

The hat stand

This is made by crumpling pasted paper sheets and covering with pasted strips to hold the rough, basic shape of head and shoulders. String may be used to tie the model into position until dry. When hard you have a firm shape, and it will be easy to apply further pasted paper to obtain the size and shape you want. Noses and other facial details are not essential, but do add interest if the stand is to be in your bedroom.

Fig. 88 *Milliner's stand* by Betty Lorrimar. Modelled with sheets of crumpled, pasted paper. The basic shape was loosly formed, allowed to dry and then covered with one or two layers of small strips, then painted with poster colours and varnished

Umbrella stands, wastepaper baskets

A piece of firm cardboard is necessary as a base for your model. This is curved after cutting it according to the height and width required. The seam is joined with brown gummed paper or Sellotape (Scotch tape) (fig. 89). Do not overlap the edges of the cardboard, or you will get a ridge and your circle will be pushed out of shape. The cylinder is placed over another piece of cardboard and a circle drawn round the bottom. This is then cut out and joined with gummed tape. Another method of making a base is to apply gummed strips of paper over one end of the cardboard. These should be put across first in one direction and the next layer in the other, so that an even thickness is obtained.

The main body of the cylinder is now covered with layers of pasted newspaper. Build up in stages; that is, allow to dry after about six layers. This will help to maintain the shape and will prevent warping. The newspaper should be put on both the outside and inside of the form. The number of layers will depend on the individual requirements. Obviously an umbrella stand needs to be thicker than a wastepaper basket, as it will have to support umbrellas. When dry and hard, and of the required thickness, you

Fig. 89 The method of joining the cardboard cylinder with strips of gummed tape before covering with papier maché

Fig. 90 *Umbrella stand* by Betty Lorrimar. The cardboard cylinder was covered with about twelve layers of papier maché. Decoration was by découpage. Covers of magazines were used to form the background, and then smaller cut-out shapes were superimposed to break up the surface

can decorate either by using coloured cut-outs from magazines or by painting.

Smaller or larger cylinders for other useful purposes can be made in this way. For instance you can make canisters for holding kitchen spoons or containers for paint brushes and pencils.

Fig. 91 *Pedlers* by Gillian Vallis and Ann Watts, aged 13. A delightful couple, dressed in subtle colours and with good use of textures. The idea was an original one, and there is great appeal in the way it has been carried out. The shawl was specially knitted for the lady. The basket was made from plaited (braided) string

Lampshades

Papier maché can be used to make many types of lampshades. One easy way is to work over a balloon. This produces a spherical shape. The balloon is first blown up to the desired size and tied. Four or five layers of tissue paper are then pasted over. A hole should be left at the top and bottom. You may use different colours or the same one, chosen to match your decoration. The paper will overlap, and give varied and interesting effects which will produce a free pattern. When the paper is dry, puncture the balloon. Trim the two open circles and tidy if necessary. The top one will prevent the bulb heat becoming too intense. The lower hole can be made to fit your lamp base and will vary accordingly.

A lampshade can also be made to fit round a bought frame. Tissue paper is pasted onto a sheet of white cartridge (drawing) paper. One layer is sufficient, but more may be used if a stronger colour is wanted. When dry brush on a coat of clear paper varnish. Make sure the tissue is really dry before doing this, as white, opaque patches are caused if it is not. Bind the frame with white tape. Cut out the lampshade pattern. You can test this by cutting it out in newspaper first and trying it on the frame. The transparent tissue pattern is now stuck with strong white adhesive onto the lampshade frame. The lampshade base may also be made of papier maché, as long as provision is made for the electrical fitting. Lamp fittings are sold in most stores selling electric components, or in crafts shops.

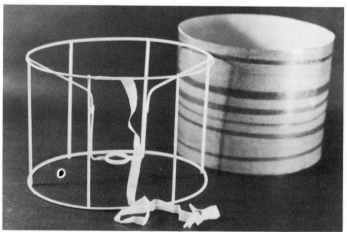

Fig. 92   The frame is bound with white tape so that the shade is easily attached. The papier-maché shade behind is waiting to be fixed onto it

Furniture

Eighteenth-century papier-maché furniture is now highly valued, and much is to be seen in antique shops and museums. It is very strong and durable, as is witnessed by the fact that it is seen in such excellent condition today and that many people still use it.

Little modern work exists in this field, which is a great pity as it is a cheap, strong and pliable material. Furniture can be made by using either pulp or layered paper.

Obviously more time and patience is called for, as the work must be done in stages. Tables, chairs and stools are among the pieces that one can make. Screens, shelves and mirror frames are also suitable subjects. As it is the creative possibilities of papier maché that this book hopes to stimulate, the examples shown are not traditionally designed. Why bother to reproduce plain styles that can be bought in any furniture store!

The coffee table (fig. 95) is a mixture of methods. The top is made of many layers of pasted sheets of newspaper. This was left on a flat surface until it was hard and dry. The legs are four figures modelled with pulp paper over a base of rolled tubes, as when making small figures (see page 38). They were joined to the top with papier-maché pulp and strips. This was not done until they were hard. They could have been screwed into position from the top. When dry the whole thing was turned over so that the figures supported the table. At this stage adjustments were made — feet padded with pulp to make them level, modelling tidied up and so on. The table was then given a coat of white emulsion paint before decorating.

The child's chair (fig. 94) was made by using layered sheets of pasted paper. The shapes were curved before it was quite dry. The various parts were sawn to the sizes and shapes required and were screwed together. Most paper originates from wood, so that it is not strange to find that it reverts to such a strong material when pulped and mixed with paste. The advantage for the home papier-maché furniture maker is the fact that curved shapes can be easily obtained. This is difficult when using wood.

Old picture frames and mirror surrounds can be renovated with papier maché. This is easier than trying to repair with wood, and after painting or covering with gold leaf it is impossible to notice the repair.

Fig. 93   Hat on hat stand by Margaret Hickson and Betty Lorrimar. The hat is from the same pattern as shown on page 81. It is decorated by the batik method described on page 18.

Fig. 94 *Chair* by Margaret Hickson. This novelty chair was made for a small girl.
It is quite strong and is attractively decorated

Fig. 95   *Coffee table* by Betty Lorrimar. The table is very firm, and makes an unusual addition to a room

Fig. 96 Bedstead, papier maché with lacquered brass mounts. This was made in
Birmingham, *c*. 1850. Victoria and Albert Museum, London

Origin and uses of papier maché

The art of papier maché has long been practised in the East, but the exact place of origin and when it was first used is not known. Its invention has been attributed to both Italy and France. Frederick the Great, who had a keen eye to business as well as an admiration for all things French, established a factory for it in Berlin in 1765. This flourished for a time and may have been the ancestor of German firms who sent papier-maché goods to the London Exhibition of 1851.

Paper was not as cheap as it is now, and it is thought that the idea of using mashed-up paper was suggested by the huge quantities of waste accumulated when notices and posters were torn down each day to make room for fresh ones in early eighteenth-century Paris. After serving its original purpose it was used to make small articles, such as snuff boxes, trinket and work boxes, which were moulded or turned from dry pulp. They were painted quite artistically.

The process died out for a few years but was revived in 1830.

It was used quite widely in early eighteenth-century England. Henry Clay, a Birmingham japanner, used the material for tray making, and for panels for coaches, doors and furniture. He pasted several sheets of paper, one over the other, placing them between boards or metal plates of regular thickness to avoid one side contracting. He then trimmed the edges and dried the sheets in a hot stove. During the drying process they were rubbed or dipped in oil or varnish. Afterwards they were rasped and pumiced to obtain a smooth surface. More sheets were applied, and the process repeated until the required thickness was obtained.

The business was very lucrative and firms were also established in Wolverhampton and London. Some used a substance called fibrous slab, which may have been paper made from vegetable matter such as hay, straw, nettles and tree bark.

The London firms Jackson and Son, and C. F. Bielfield, issued large illustrated catalogues of uses to which the material could be put. It was a useful substitute for plaster in moulded ornaments on ceilings and walls. After the fire of 1834 the mouldings and ceilings in the House of Lords were made of the material.

Bielfields made furniture, carriages and even houses from papier maché. It is known that ten cottages and a ten-roomed villa made by the firm were exported to Australia in 1853. It is not known whether they still exist!

Henry Clay made Sedan chairs, panels for rooms, doors, bookcases, tables and ships' cabins. Paper can be composed of many materials. If made from wood pulp, one can understand its strength when mixed with glues and oils. Another type is made from rags, old bags and sacking. This makes an ideal pulp for tea-trays and screens.

Fig. 97   Persian writing box. Kalemdan, painted with battle scenes, Nineteenth century. Victoria and Albert Museum, London

In printing, moulds were (and still are in places) made from papier maché. Pasted sheets of blotting paper were laid onto a brown backing paper. A few sheets of tissue paper formed the top layers. The printer would then take an impression from the type by beating or by heavy pressure. He could then make a cast from it. The flexibility of the material enabled him to bend it for casting on curved plates and thus use a rotary press.

Many other uses were found for papier maché. Toys were made, dolls' heads, lay figures, milliners' and clothiers' blocks, mirror and picture frames, boxes and small domestic articles.

The material is much used in folk art, religious processions and rites. In India beautifully-decorated cows are modelled and later burnt as part of a Hindu ceremony.

Fig. 98   Chinese nodding-head tiger, c. 1900. Museum of Childhood, Edinburgh

Fig. 99   Tray used by parlour maids. It has shell inlay and gilt ornament on a black
ground 1865. Victoria and Albert Museum, London

Fig. 100 Making a festival figure for a Durga Puja ceremony. The models are papier maché and are decorated with foil, cut paper work and jewels. They are colourful and rich in elaborate design

In Mexico huge Judas figures are made to be used in processions. They are used at Easter and are on sale beforehand in the capital. They vary in size, and can be very small or larger than life-size. These images may represent well-known personalities who are unpopular, or death — often symbolized by skeletons or grotesque devils. The large ones are filled with fireworks and are either burnt or blown-up on Easter Saturday. At fiestas, too, the Mexicans use papier-maché models, which are artistically decorated and filled or covered with fireworks.

Pinatas are made at Christmas. These are gay animals or birds which are traditionally suspended from the ceiling to hold Christmas gifts.

Beautiful examples of papier maché are to be found in China, Japan, India and Burma. In China it was used before it was discovered in Europe and America. Chinese soldiers wore helmets made of the substance, as it was light to wear and easy to make.

Persia and Kashmir were also famous for the artistic objects made from papier maché.

Today there are quite a few artists producing exciting papier-maché models.

Fig. 101   Spirit case painted and inlaid with mother-of-pearl, 1860. Victoria and Albert Museum, London

Fig. 102 *Grandit, je t'aaplatis* by Niki de Saint-Phalle. Sculpture in various materials. 67 ins high (170 cms). Photo Hanover Gallery, London

Modern sculptors are treating papier maché as a serious and useful material. Its freedom and possibilities are being used more and more. One of the pioneers of the modern approach to sculpture, Alexander Archipenko — carried out serious compositions in the medium. Like the other Cubist and Futurist sculptors in the first quarter of the century, he experimented with a great variety of materials to express his ideas.

Elie Nadelman, the Polish sculptor, also made interesting constructions in the medium. He was a serious student of folk art and this probably helped to influence his choice of material.

Niki de Saint-Phalle has made a series of *Nanas* using papier-maché. They are charming, simplified female figures, often painted in bold colours.

Papier maché is being used more and more by graphic designers, in an effort to achieve a lively effect, such as one can attain when working in three dimensions. Models are being made and then photographed for book covers, posters and illustrations.

In the classroom it can be a most useful substance. Teachers never seem to be allowed enough money to spend on materials and equipment. Papier maché is easily obtained and cheap. It is a material that is well worth exploring to produce really imaginative results.

Fig. 103   *Hula girl*   by Fiona Taylor and Lynn Young, aged 14. This colourful life size figure is painted chocolate brown. Her hair is black wool (yarn) which has been combed. The flowers are of tissue paper. Her sarong was decorated by the tie and dye method (see page 19)

Fig. 104 *Noah's Ark*. Group work by eleven year olds. Each child had a part in making Noah and the ark. Some made animals, some human figures, and others were busy building the ark. The subject is a good one, as there is a job for everyone. This photograph shows the boat and some of the early arrivals.

Opposite
Fig. 105 *Girl reading* by Janet West, aged 11. A small figure expressively sitting on her cardboard chair. Her hair is unravelled yellow wool (yarn)

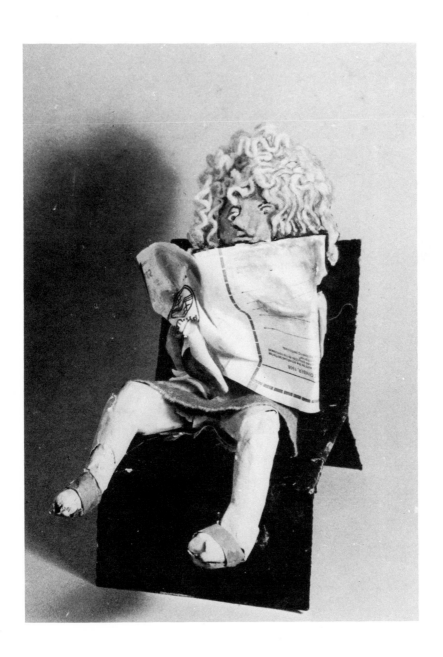

List of suppliers

Cellulose and other pastes, emulsion paint, enamels, lacquers and varnish, Copydex and other synthetic white glues, wire
Home decorating suppliers, Woolworths, hardware stores

Watercolour paints, acrylic and oil paints, brushes, gummed tape, gesso
Any good art materials store

Findings for earrings, cuff-links, bracelets etc.
Handicrafts shops.
In U.S. may be ordered by mail from T. B. Hagstoz and Son, 709 Sansom Street, Philadelphia, Pennsylvania 19106

Oil of cloves, dextrin
Chemists.
In U.S. pharmacies (you may have to try pharmacies which specialize in the out-of-the-ordinary item.) May be ordered by mail from Caswell-Massey Co. Ltd, 114 East 25th Street, New York, NY 10010

Picture hangers (passe partout rings)
Picture framing shops, hardware stores

Papier maché is one of the least costly crafts, so that very little expenditure is required. Most people have many of the materials they need and can use up left-overs from home decorating, in a pleasant way.

Fur further reading

Crafts Design by Spencer Moseley, Pauline Johnson and Hazel Koenig; Wadsworth Publishing Co., California 1962

Decorative Arts of Asia and Egypt by H. T. Bossert; Praeger, New York 1956

Découpage by Patricia Nimrocks; Charles Scribner's Sons, New York 1968

Die Fabrikation der Papier Maché und Papierstoff by L. E. Andes; Waaren, Vienna 1900

Exploring Papier Maché by Victoria B. Betts; Davis Publications, New York 1955

Mexican Folk Art by Gerd Dörner; Wilhelm Anderman Verlag, Munich 1962

Papier Maché and How to Use It by Mildred Anderson; Oak Tree Press, London; Sterling Publishing Co., Inc., New York 1965

Primitive Art by Frank Boaz; Thames and Hudson London 1962; Dover Publications, New York 1955

The Art of Papier Maché by Carla and John B. Kenny; Chilton, London and New York 1968

The Folk Arts of Japan by Hugo Munsterberg; Charles E. Tuttle Co., 1958

The Magic of a People by Alexander Girard; Viking Press, New York 1968

Index

Adhesives 9, 10

Beads 74
Book list 103
Bottle figures 30
Boxes 78
Bracelets 74
Brooches 74–5

Cellulose paste 9
Chairs 87
Cylinders 84

Découpage 13
Dolls 76

Earrings 74
Emulsion paint 12

Figures 38
Flour paste 9
Flowers 71
Furniture 87

Gesso 10
Glues 10

Hat stands 83
Hats 80

Jewellery 73

Lampshades 86

Maracas 26
Marionettes 66
Masks 60
Montage 13
Moulding 20

Paints 9, 12
Paste 9
Pendants 74
Pulp 52
Puppets 64

Rings 4

Scenery 67
Sculpture 55
Stage properties 67
Suppliers 102

Tables 87
Toys 36
Trays 28
Trompe d'oeil 13

Umbrella stand 84

Wastepaper baskets 84

Rings 74

General Editors Brenda Herbert and Janey O'Riordan
Set in 9 point Univers
Manufactured by Parish Press, Inc.